WHAT GOES ON INSIDE YOUR BRAIN?

LANGUAGE, COMMUNICATION, AND YOUR BRAIN

ROBYN HARDYMAN

Gareth Stevens Publishing

Please visit our website, **www.garethstevens.com**.
For a free color catalog of all our high-quality books,
call toll free 1-800-542-2595 or fax 1-877-542-2596.

Cataloging-in-Publication Data
Names: Hardyman, Robyn.
Title: Language, communication, and your brain / Robyn Hardyman.
Description: New York : Gareth Stevens Publishing, 2019. | Series: What goes on inside your brain? | Includes glossary and index.
Identifiers: ISBN 9781538235607 (pbk.) | ISBN 9781538235614 (library bound)
Subjects: LCSH: Language and languages--Juvenile literature. | Communication--Juvenile literature. | Brain--Juvenile literature.
Classification: LCC P107.H378 2019 | DDC 808'.0427--dc23

First Edition

Published in 2019 by
Gareth Stevens Publishing
111 East 14th Street, Suite 349
New York, NY 10003

Produced by Calcium
Editors: Sarah Eason and Claudia Martin
Designers: Paul Myerscough and Jeni Child

Photo credits: Cover: Shutterstock/John Warner. Inside: Database Center for Life Science (DCLS)/Body Parts 3D: p.13; Mariano: p.39; Shutterstock: Alila Medical Media: p.24; anekoho: p.9, p.22; BestPhotoStudio: p.20; Claudio Divizia: p.6; Daniel M Ernst: p.12; decade3d/anatomy online: p.27, p.33; dwphotos: p.38; Elena Veselova: p.8; gmstockstudio: p.11; Gorodenkoff: p.43; Image Point Fr: p.19; Jacob Lund: p.34; jorik: p.44; Kamira: p.32; Koe Sze Kiat: p.1; Lazarenko Svetlana: p.37; Leszek Glasner: p.18; Lilly Trott: p.35; LStockStudio: p.15; Marcos Mesa Sam Worsley: p.29; Maria Symchych: p.23; Mariia Masich: p.36; Monkey Business Images: p.7, p.16; Mukesh Kumar Jwala: p.40; Ollyy: p.3, p.26; oneinchpunch: p.4; pathdoc: p.14; Phonlamai Photo: p.42; Photobac: p.30; photographee.eu: p.25; pikselstock: p.10; Simone van den Berg: p.17; SpeedKingz: p.45; Studio Grand Ouest: p.28; Syda Productions: p.31; tsuneomp: p.5; wavebreakmedia: p.21; Zivika Kerkez: p.41.

Printed in the United States of America.

CPSIA compliance information: Batch #CW19GS
For further information contact Gareth Stevens, New York, New York at 1-800-542-2595.

CONTENTS

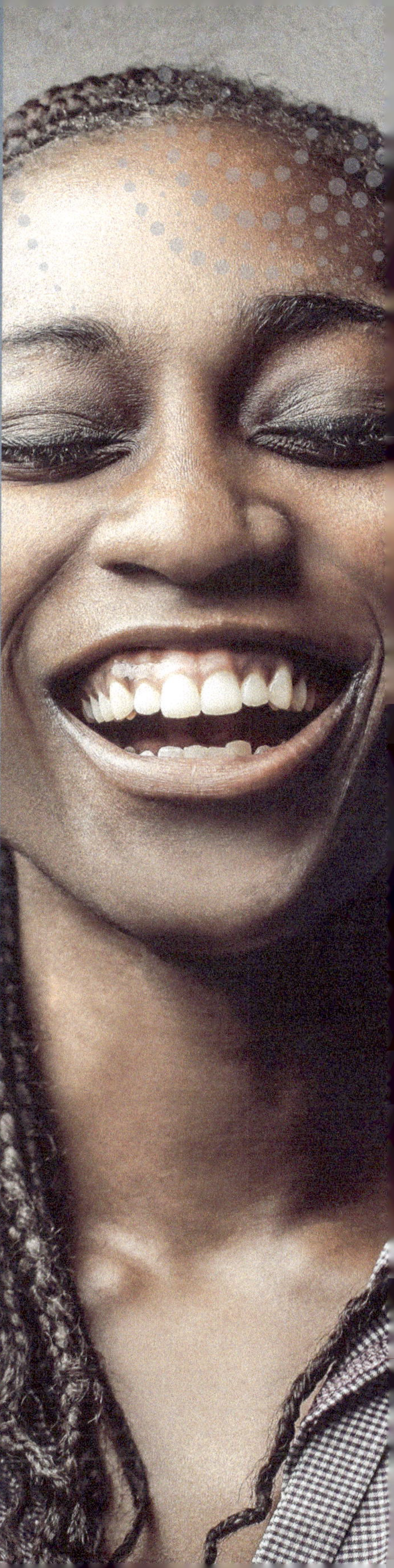

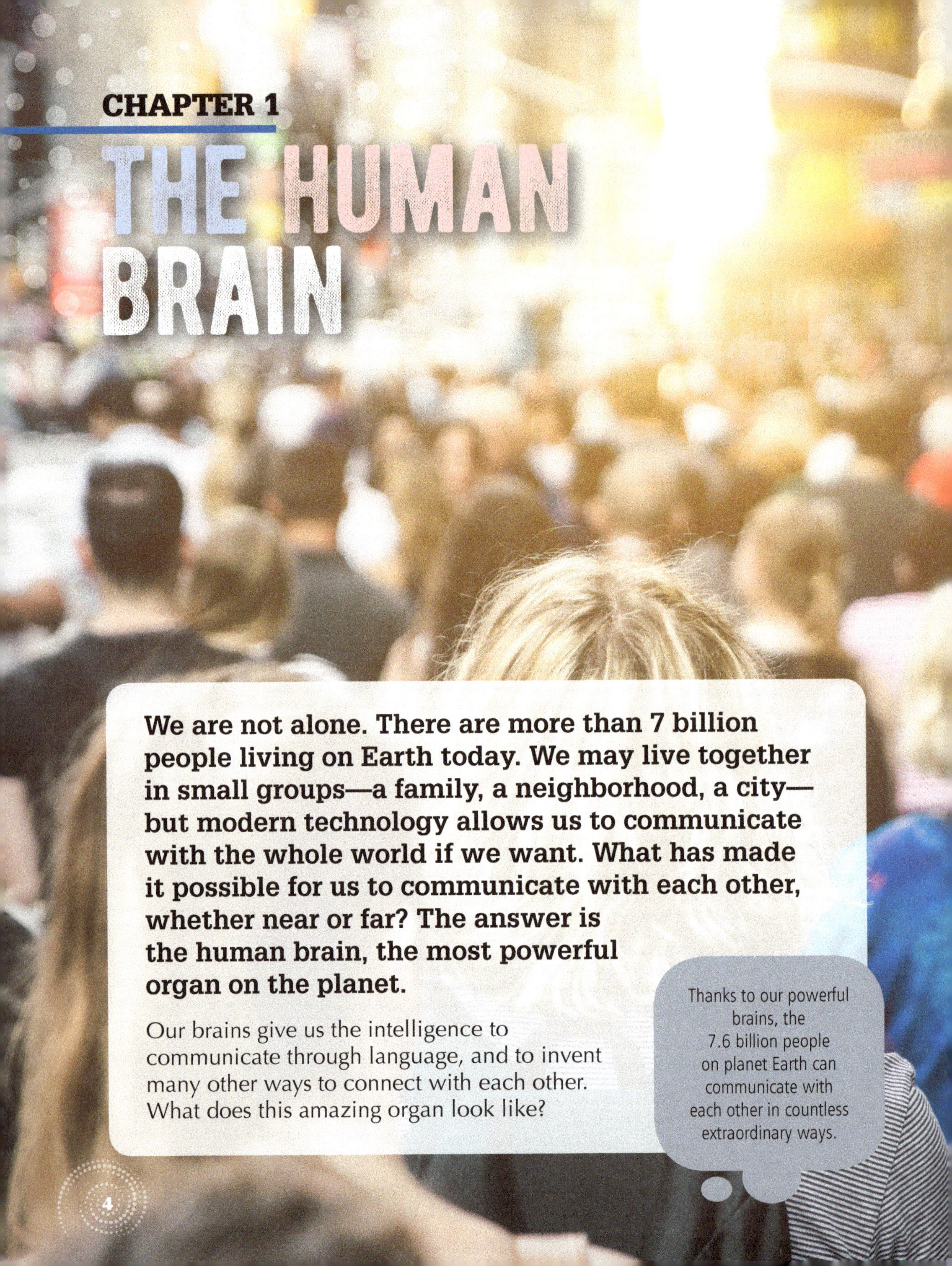

CHAPTER 1

THE HUMAN BRAIN

We are not alone. There are more than 7 billion people living on Earth today. We may live together in small groups—a family, a neighborhood, a city—but modern technology allows us to communicate with the whole world if we want. What has made it possible for us to communicate with each other, whether near or far? The answer is the human brain, the most powerful organ on the planet.

Our brains give us the intelligence to communicate through language, and to invent many other ways to connect with each other. What does this amazing organ look like?

Thanks to our powerful brains, the 7.6 billion people on planet Earth can communicate with each other in countless extraordinary ways.

It is about the size of two fists put together, and its surface is gray and deeply wrinkled. It is divided into two equal halves, called the right and left hemispheres. The surface layer is called the cerebral cortex. This is where most of our thinking happens, as well as movement, memory, and language.

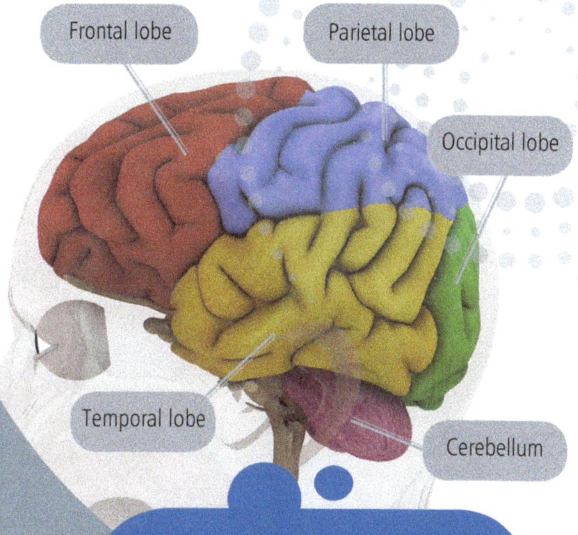

Each hemisphere is divided into four lobes, each of which is associated with different functions.

Each half of the brain is divided into four main regions, called lobes. The frontal lobe is behind your forehead, the parietal lobe is on the top of your head, the temporal lobes are at the sides, and the occipital lobe is at the back. Different processes happen in different lobes, such as remembering facts or processing input from the senses. Scientists think that the areas of the brain we use when we hear speech are in the temporal lobes, on each side of our head. Deep inside the brain, below the lobes, are other structures that control our most basic actions. The cerebellum controls the working of our muscles, and the brain stem controls our heartbeat and breathing.

INSIDE YOUR BRAIN

As we grow and learn, the connections between neurons grow, too, making the brain's network more complex. As new connections are made, old ones are strengthened by being used over and over. As we learn and practice a skill, such as speaking, the pathway in the network that allows us to do that gets stronger, until we can perform that skill easily.

Neurons

The brain is made of nerve cells, or neurons. Each one has long tentacles, which it uses to connect to lots of other neurons. There are about 100 billion neurons in your brain, each with up to 10,000 connections, and together they form an incredible network, an advanced information superhighway. Neurons send messages to each other as electrical signals, at up to 250 miles per hour (400 km/h). Trillions of signals are being sent around your brain every second.

The Rosetta Stone allowed us to solve the puzzle of ancient Egyptian hieroglyphics.

An Advanced Species

The creatures of the natural world have developed many remarkable ways of communicating with one another. Birds and whales, for example, use song to send messages between members of their species. Human beings are alone, however, in having developed an amazingly complex and flexible means of communicating—spoken and written language.

It is our sophisticated methods of communication, powered by our extraordinary brains, that have made us such an advanced species. Over thousands of years, they have allowed us to develop rich cultures, to investigate the world, and to pass on what we have learned. Being able to speak to each other allows us to exchange information very quickly and accurately. At the most basic level of survival, when faced with a danger we can yell, "Look out! Car coming on your left!" Beyond that, we can ask questions at all levels of seriousness: "Would you like chocolate chip or strawberry ice cream?" or "What do you think is the meaning of life?" Questions spark debate, and so we learn from each other. As well as passing on facts, we can tell each other stories, express our hopes, and explain our feelings.

Past and Future

Our language even allows us to communicate with the generations of people who lived before us, and the generations that will follow us, because we can write down information about our lives, and so preserve it. Without written language we would know much less about our history. The Rosetta Stone was found in Egypt in 1799. In 196 BCE, it was carved with the same information in three languages: ancient Greek, an ancient Egyptian form of writing called Demotic script, and Egyptian hieroglyphics, which is made up of picture-like symbols. Experts could translate the Greek, but they could not understand the Egyptian writing. Using the Greek on the Rosetta Stone, they were able to figure out how Demotic and hieroglyphics worked, and as a result they discovered much about the amazing richness of the ancient Egyptian world.

SPEAK YOUR MIND

Think about all the forms of written communication we use to find out about the past, such as government records, newspapers, people's personal letters and diaries, as well as novels, plays, and biographies. What pieces of your own writing do you think could be useful to historians of the future? Give reasons for your answer.

Recording your activities and thoughts in a diary will create a record that you, and possibly future generations, can read in many years' time.

CHAPTER 2

THINKING

To be able to communicate, you have to think. Thinking is really just another name for the whizzing of electrical signals around the billions of networks in your brain. Over the years of your life so far, you have created the pathways in your brain that allow you to hear a question, understand it, decide on your reply, and deliver it with your voice. We can do all that in a split second!

When you are asked about your ice cream preference, you have to think before you say, "Strawberry, please." The part of the brain that allows us to think is the cerebral cortex, the outer, deeply

It's the cerebral cortex that allows you to see those ice cream flavors, choose which you like, and ask for it!

wrinkled layer. It receives signals from our senses, such as our eyes and ears, and processes them. Different areas of the cortex are sent into action by different kinds of signal. For example, it is the occipital lobes, at the back of the head, that process signals from your eyes—so these lobes receive the information about what each of those ice cream flavors looks like, then pass it on through countless neural networks! Much of your conscious thinking happens in the frontal lobe, which is located just behind your forehead. This is the part of your brain you use for reasoning things through, for planning, and for figuring out what you are going to do—like choose strawberry ice cream! This is perhaps where our advanced human "intelligence" resides.

In evolutionary terms, humans are quite closely related to chimpanzees, but there is a huge difference in brain and language capacity.

Human vs. Chimp

Your brain's cortex is about four times as big as the brain of a chimp in its surface area. Your head is bigger than a chimp's, but not four times bigger. Your bigger brain can fit inside your head because your cortex is much more folded over and wrinkled, allowing it to fit in a relatively small space in your skull.

INSIDE YOUR BRAIN

Parts of the brain can survive intact when other parts are harmed, causing terrible loss of function in the rest of the body. Sometimes people suffer from "locked-in syndrome" after a very serious stroke in their brain makes their body paralyzed. They cannot move or speak, but they can still think. One man who suffered this agonizing experience managed to write a book about it from the prison of his body. All he could move was one eyelid, so he learned to blink out letters to another person and, over a very long time, tell the world about the thoughts that were going on in his conscious brain.

Our unconscious brains help us form first impressions of people, often within just a few seconds of meeting them.

Unconscious Thinking

A large amount of our thinking is unconscious, meaning it happens without us being aware of it. For example, when you walk you do not think, "I'm going to put my left foot forward, now my right, now my left," and so on. It happens automatically. Once you have learned the skill of walking, and many, many others, you can do it with your unconscious brain.

The brain is superfast at unconscious thinking. It takes in signals from the outside world, or remembers things it has learned and stored away in the memory, then makes decisions and tells the body how to respond, even before we are aware of having had a thought at all! We use the unconscious brain a lot when we are communicating with each other. Once we have learned to speak, for example, we can make the sounds that create the words of our language, without thinking carefully about them. Similarly, once we know how to write, we can form the letters and spell the words of our language automatically. We may need to nudge the brain a little to remember a spelling sometimes, but mostly we write without much conscious thought.

First Impressions

Our unconscious brain plays an important role in nonverbal communications, too. When we meet someone for the first time, we take in all kinds of information about them without being aware of it.

We make judgments about whether a person seems friendly or threatening, trustworthy or unreliable, all within a few seconds. It may seem unfair that the size of your eyes, the shape of your face, or the way you are standing should influence how people react to you, but we simply cannot help it. Once we start communicating in more regular ways, by talking for example, we can show our personality in a more reassuring way.

SPEAK YOUR MIND

Sometimes we get the feeling that "something is wrong." This kind of gut feeling is called intuition, and it usually becomes stronger as we get older. Intuition is a form of unconscious thinking, and it is surprising how often it turns out to be correct. Can you think why intuition becomes more common and stronger in people who are older? Give reasons for your answers.

Our experiences in life teach us about situations that may not be safe. As we get older, we develop a stronger sense of intuition.

CHAPTER 3

LANGUAGE

You know you can tell stories and jokes, ask questions, shout instructions on the sports field, and whisper secrets in a friend's ear, but what exactly is language? Spoken language is a collection of coded sounds. There are almost 7,000 languages spoken around the world. Each one has a different system for coding sounds to create words with meaning. How do we learn to master this extraordinary skill?

Being able to communicate with our friends and family using language is one of the great joys of life.

Babies hear the sound of their mother's voice while in the womb, and ultrasound scans show they can respond to it. As soon as a baby is born, he or she recognizes the sound of the mother's voice, but cannot talk or understand words. The communication is nonverbal, but the baby soon starts to learn from interactions with people. A six-month-old babbling baby is trying to copy the sounds of speech. The baby is making the sounds that form a language, but has not learned the coding system yet! These sounds are called phonemes. All over the world, babies of a few months old make the same sounds. By the time they are one year old, they are making the sounds of their native language. By age two, they can say quite a few words.

Broca's and Wernicke's Areas

The processes involved in understanding speech and making it are separate and happen in two different brain areas. These areas are mainly located in two regions, called Broca's and Wernicke's areas. They are both usually in the left hemisphere of the brain, although occasionally these enlarged regions develop in the right side, particularly among left-handed people. Together, these brain regions, and the nerve connections between them, form a network that provides the hardware for language in the brain.

INSIDE YOUR BRAIN

Broca's area is a region in the frontal lobe that is responsible for producing speech. It is named for the French doctor Paul Broca, who discovered it in the 1870s. It is here that the instructions are generated for making speech sounds. As babies grow, so Broca's area develops, too, until finally young children are able to make the sounds of words that people around them can understand.

Broca's area and Wernicke's area are usually in the brain's left hemisphere. Broca's area is responsible for producing speech, while Wernicke's area is responsible for understanding it.

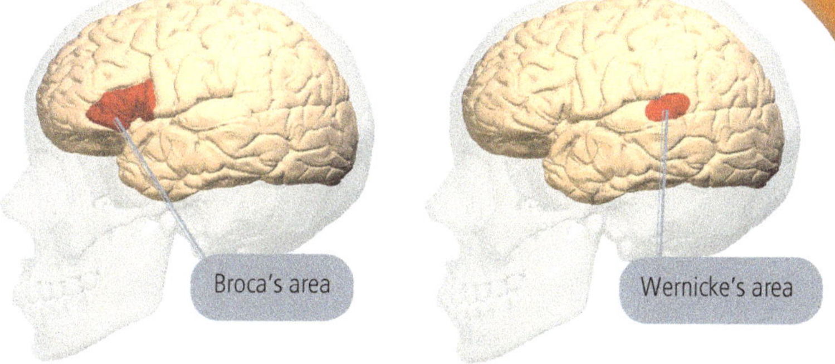

Understanding

It is all very well being able to make the sounds of words, but spoken language is not much use to us if we cannot understand it. If you travel to a country where people speak a language you do not know, it can feel quite disturbing not being able to follow anything that is happening around you. We can tell that the sounds of people's speech are part of a language, but our brains cannot decode them. How, then, do we learn to do this in our own language?

Our understanding of spoken and written language happens in a specific area of the brain called Wernicke's area. Without it, words and sentences would be nothing more than a jumble of sounds.

The part of the brain we use for understanding language is at the back of the temporal lobe in the left hemisphere, and it is called Wernicke's area, after a scientist named Carl Wernicke who discovered it in the 1880s. We use this area to understand both spoken and written language. Experiments have shown that, when we hear a spoken language we know, this part of the brain processes the signals from the ear and, at first, recognizes the sounds. Then it recognizes that these sounds are making words, and finally it recognizes the meaning of those words. Of course, all this happens incredibly quickly, in a split second, so that we seem to hear the words and understand them instantly.

When a parent reads a story to a child, both the reader and listener are using the same area in their brains to understand the story.

Listening to Stories

In an interesting experiment, one person read a story aloud to another person who listened, while both their brains were monitored. The brain responses in both the reader and the listener were in the same areas and followed a very similar pattern. The speaker was using the same part of their brain to understand the story as they read it aloud, as the listener was using to understand it by hearing.

SPEAK YOUR MIND

If a person suffered damage to the Wernicke's area of their brain, how do you think their language would be affected? Remember that this is the area responsible for understanding language, rather than for producing it. Do you think they would still be able to talk normally? Give reasons for your answers.

Being Bilingual

For many children, the language spoken at home with their family is different than the language primarily spoken in the country where they live. This can be great for these kids, as they get to develop language super-skills. The easiest time for your brain to learn another language is when you are very young. From about six months old, babies start to zone in on the sounds of the language they hear most, and begin to learn it. If exposed to a second language at this stage, a baby will also begin to learn that one, using the same area of the brain. The pathways of neurons in the "language-learning" area of the brain will become strong, particularly in Broca's area. The child grows up bilingual, which means a person can speak two languages equally well. The really great thing about this is that the child will generally also find it easier to learn other languages throughout life.

Growing up in a family where two languages are spoken fluently gives you great language-learning skills.

Older Learners

Most people learn new languages when they are a little older, often in school. Bilingual people who learned another language when very young use one Broca's area for speaking both their native languages. However, people who learn a second language later actually develop two distinct Broca's areas. These areas are very close together, but divided. Brain scans have shown that, when the person speaks one language, they use one part of their Broca's area, then when they switch to the other language, they use the other.

The best years to learn new languages are up to the age of about 20. After that, the brain finds it more difficult to establish strong pathways for learning a new language fluently. It is still quite possible to gain a good knowledge of new languages throughout your adult life, however, if you work hard at it!

INSIDE YOUR BRAIN

If a very young child's parents each speak a different language, he will find it easiest to learn them both if they each speak to him mainly in their own language. He may mix the languages in his own speech at first, but by the age of about three he will have separated the words belonging to each language and will know which one to use with which parent. By the age of about seven, he will know the grammar and vocabulary for the two languages.

The high school years are a great time to learn a new language. Although it's never too late to pick up French, or Spanish, or Chinese, it may take a little longer as you age.

When Things Go Wrong

We are so used to communicating with language that we take it for granted that everyone can understand us.

When you see a friend at the mall, you might say, "Hi! How are you? Do you want to go see that new movie this weekend?" We take it for granted that we can put our thoughts into words and communicate with other people whenever we want to. Sometimes, however, people suffer damage to their brain, and this can affect their ability both to speak and to understand language. As language forms such an important part of our daily life, this can be very challenging for them.

The loss of the ability to speak is called aphasia. Aphasia is often the result of a person having a stroke, or "brain attack," where the blood flow to the brain is interrupted for a while. It can also be caused by an infection or by a tumor in the brain. Damage in different areas causes different kinds of aphasia. So, for example, if the region known as Wernicke's area is damaged, the person's understanding of language is affected. They are still able to speak fluently, to form words and sentences that are grammatically correct, but the things they say do not make sense, because their understanding is impaired.

If the damage occurs in Broca's area, the aphasia affects the person's ability to speak. They will struggle to find words to express what they want to say, even though their understanding is not impaired. They will use simple vocabulary, and speak very slowly, with long pauses between single words.

Speech Therapies

People with aphasia can be helped by speech and language therapies. Expert therapists design their therapies to match the person's type of aphasia. So for Broca's aphasia, they work with patients on improving their ability to find the words they want and to say them in full sentences, and for Wernicke's aphasia they work on improving the patient's understanding so they can speak with more meaning. Family members and other caregivers can help, too, by supporting the therapist's work with regular speech exercises and lots of practice.

Speech and language therapists can really help people who suffer from difficulties with language. Sometimes, adults have to learn how to speak all over again.

SPEAK YOUR MIND

If a person is suffering from Broca's aphasia and has difficulty finding words, how do you think you could help them when you speak with them? Think about the speed and clarity of what you say, and about other possible ways of communicating with them. Give reasons for your answers.

CHAPTER 4

READING AND WRITING

As you read this book, the electrical signals are whizzing around the networks of neurons across your brain. But how exactly does your eyes seeing the letters "b-r-a-i-n" set off the chain of brainwaves that results in you thinking the word "brain" and knowing what that means? Reading—and writing—are extraordinary skills that many of us take for granted, once we have mastered them!

Messages from your eyes are processed in the occipital lobe. Ever since you started learning to read, you have been building up your memory bank of words:

The process of reading starts when visual signals from our eyes reach the occipital lobe at the back of the brain.

Learning to write is a complex skill that takes years of practice to master.

what they look like and what they mean. In an unbelievably short time, your brain recognizes that the letters "b-r-a-i-n" spell the word "brain," and that the word means the organ inside your head that controls your body and allows you to think. Not only that, but it starts on the next word, and the next, long before you even realize you are reading.

People with impaired sight use a different reading system. Although the initial sensory input comes from touch rather than sight, the process of reading is similar. Braille is a system of raised dots that represent letters, and blind people learn to read these with their fingers.

Learning to Write

When you want to write a word, another extraordinary process takes place. Once we have learned how to spell a word, our brain extracts that information from our memory, and sends signals through our nervous system to the muscles in our hands, telling them how to form the shapes of the letters while holding a pen. You probably remember learning to write, and how your letters looked wobbly at first. It's no wonder, because this is a very advanced skill. It takes several years of practice for us to be able to write neatly and to join up our letters. Learning to spell well takes even longer, but that is all about memory.

INSIDE YOUR BRAIN

As complex a task as reading is, thanks to developments in neuroscience and technology, scientists can now identify the areas and neural pathways the brain uses for doing it. Several areas of the brain work together, like performers in an orchestra. The temporal lobe decodes the sounds of letters and words, while the frontal lobe handles reading fluency, grammar, and comprehension. A third area, in the parietal lobe, acts as a "conductor" for the orchestra, linking the action from the other areas.

How Children Learn to Read

The science behind how we learn to read is incredibly complex. We are the only species that has the brainpower to develop this amazing skill, so it must take a lot of activity in the brain, over a long period of time, to master it. Neuroscientists, who study the physical aspects of the brain, and psychologists, who study how we think and learn, work together to uncover how we develop this capability. This is really important, because it helps educators teach children how to read in the most effective way, and how to help the children who find reading difficult.

Learning to read involves many different skills. First, we learn and memorize the smallest units of sound, called phonemes. These can be from a single letter, like "p," or a collection of letters, like the "oo" in "book," the "ee" in "knee," or the "sh" in "ship." Then we learn to blend the sounds, to put them together to make words. Of course, English is a pretty complex language, and the phonemes can be confusing, but your amazing brain eventually learns that, for example, the letters "ch" can create the different phonemes used in the words "chef," "school," and "chip."

Gradually, our fluency improves. All the time, our memory is storing away the vocabulary we learn, and our comprehension of meaning grows. Our brain's capacity for paying attention and concentrating also improves as we get older. Your classes in school now are longer and involve more work and less play than they did when you were in first grade! Your brain is maturing and you can use it to read all kinds of information.

When we learn to read, we use "phonics," or the sounds of letters, which we usually say out loud at first. Over time, we learn how to recognize whole words.

Older siblings, cousins, and friends can help a young child's capacity to read by talking with them and listening as they speak.

Reading Boost

Scientists think that there is another aspect of learning to read that has been underestimated in the past. They recognize now that children with good spoken language skills often learn to read more easily than children who are less fluent talkers. Experiments have shown that if young children are given help with their oral language before they start learning to read, they will become better readers later. This process is all about conditioning the brain to be familiar with the sounds of language, so that we recognize them easily when we see them written down.

SPEAK YOUR MIND

Speaking your mind is an essential part of learning to read! As soon as they can form words, very young children should be encouraged to talk as much as possible. How do you think parents, siblings, and others can help with this, in the routines of everyday life? Think about the importance of telling stories, of discussion, and of voicing emotions. Give reasons for your answers.

Dyslexia

Brain scans of people who are reading show us that the ability to read is one of the most complex skills we can learn in our lifetime. Most of us do master it in the end, and find we really enjoy reading. There is great pleasure in reading a gripping adventure story, or a moving poem, or an interesting article about the news. For some people, however, reading can be a struggle. The good news is that we have discovered that the brain can change and learn at any age. It can, in effect, be rewired for reading.

One of the most common reading disorders is dyslexia. Scientists think this may affect about 1 in every 10 to 20 people. People with dyslexia are no less intelligent than everyone else. They find reading difficult because their brain has trouble recognizing phonemes, the sounds that make up words, and relating them to letters. The exact cause of dyslexia is not known, but it often seems to run in families. In people with dyslexia, it is thought that certain genes inherited from their parents may act together in a way that affects how some parts of the brain develop during early life.

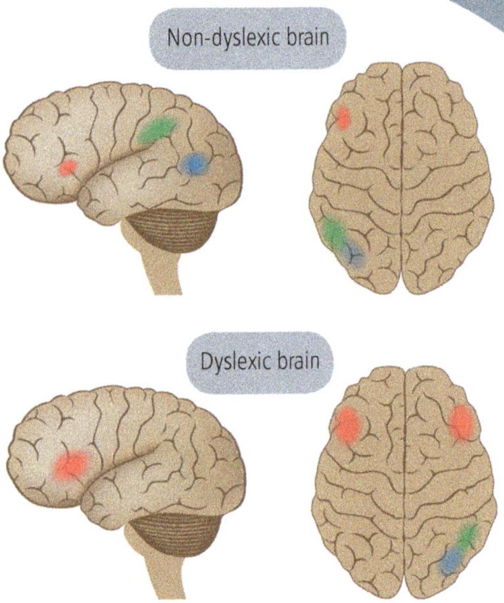

Dyslexia particularly affects the areas of the left temporal lobe that process the sounds of letters and words, shown here in red, blue, and green.

INSIDE YOUR BRAIN

Magnetic resonance imaging (MRI) scans create a picture of the inside of the brain. MRI scans have revealed that dyslexia affects the development of the left temporal lobe in the brain, the area that decodes the sounds of letters and words. The problems begin to develop as the baby's brain grows while they are still in the womb. Dyslexia cannot be cured, but specialist help can greatly improve the symptoms by rewiring the brain, especially if it is given from an early age.

Developmental Language Disorder

Another disorder that affects children's ability to learn to read and write is called developmental language disorder (DLD). DLD involves difficulty with talking and understanding language. It probably affects just as many people as dyslexia, possibly more, but it is often not recognized. Instead, children with DLD can be thought less intelligent or just badly behaved. DLD impacts the child's progress in reading and writing as much as dyslexia, but also their confidence and their ability to socialize. Brain scans of children with DLD show no particular differences from brain scans of children with average language abilities. Like dyslexia, DLD does seem to run in families, which suggests there may be a genetic cause. Some specialists think DLD may be linked with issues in the temporal lobe in processing signals from the ears, while others think it is linked with difficulties in memorizing the sounds and meanings of language.

When specialists work with children with language and reading difficulties from an early age, it can make a big difference in their progress.

CHAPTER 5

COMMUNICATING FEELINGS

So you can read, you can write, you can speak to the guy at the store to ask for a soda, and understand him when he tells you the price. This is all very practical. We are not only practical beings, however. We have feelings, too! Communicating our feelings is just as important as communicating for practical reasons, and our brains have given us some amazing ways of doing just that.

Every day, you express countless feelings, from joy to annoyance!

Of course, the place where our feelings come from is our brain! In the past, before science revealed the brain as the control center of the body and source of all thought, people used to think our emotions were caused by the imbalance between different fluids in the body! In fact, whether you are feeling full of joy or down in the dumps, it is your brain that's responsible.

The Limbic System

Our emotions may come from the brain, but they can affect our whole body. When we are sad, we may also feel weak and not much like being active, but when we are happy we may want to bounce around. Where in the brain do these emotions come from, and how do they work? The answer lies in our limbic system. This is a complex set of structures deep inside the brain, under the cerebral cortex. It includes the amygdala, which is the emotional hub of the brain. This is a very ancient part of the brain, and is similar in other, less-developed animals. The amygdala generates basic instinctive emotions, such as fear and excitement, that are important for our survival. Most of our emotions are generated unconsciously. We are not aware of deciding to feel afraid, worried, or happy. These are powerful drives that warn us of danger, or send us out in search of new experiences and opportunities.

SPEAK YOUR MIND

How much do you think people should express their emotions? Does the fact that some emotions are essential to our survival make it more important to express them? Do you think there are some emotions we should repress? Give reasons for your answers.

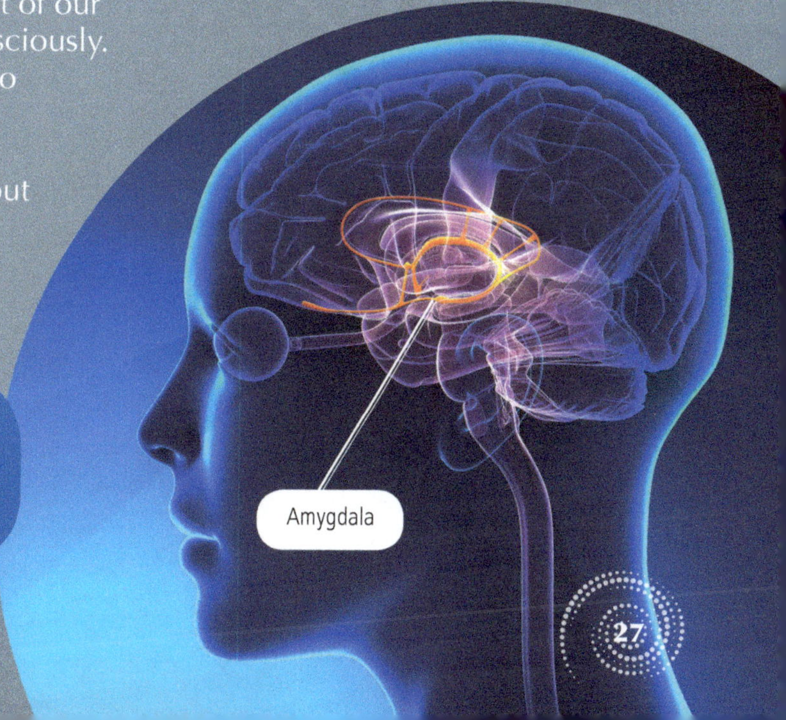

The limbic system is deep inside the brain. It includes the tiny amygdala, which is involved in many of our emotions.

Body Language

When it comes to communicating our feelings, we often use less obvious methods than spoken or written words. We have developed more subtle ways to "read" each other's thoughts, and to tell others about what is going on in our own heads, too—more subtle even than the tone of voice you use. Did you realize that your body is a powerful tool for communication? Your brain can generate some pretty strong emotions, so powerful that they are transmitted to your body all the time. You express these emotions through your body language.

Body language includes the way you stand or sit, how you hold yourself, and what you do with your eyes. If you are slouched in a chair and hardly move when your mom comes into the room, she can tell by your body language that you are not feeling responsive. A teacher can tell that the student sitting up straight in the front row of the class is eager and ready to learn. If you are feeling sad, you

Body language is often easy to read. Do you think this woman is feeling comfortable and positive?

might sit hunched over and look down. Perhaps you are trying to avoid making eye contact with others. All these signs are a very effective way of communicating with other people, but we are not usually conscious of making them. In the future, be conscious of your body language when you are with strangers or friends. Research has shown that you may unintentionally sit with your arms and legs crossed when you are feeling threatened. In contrast, when we feel a bond with someone, we may unintentionally copy their body language.

However we try to hide our feelings, our eyes often give them away.

Expressive Faces

The most expressive part of your body is your face. There are six main facial expressions that we make, and they are the same in people all around the world, whatever their ethnicity or spoken language. These are surprise, fear, sadness, anger, joy, and disgust. So wide eyes, raised eyebrows, and a wrinkled forehead, for example, will always be read as "surprise" by anyone, anywhere.

INSIDE YOUR BRAIN

Our facial expressions are part of our genetic makeup, so they are hardwired into our brains. They happen automatically, but we can learn to control them a little, if we do not want to reveal too much about how we are feeling. Mostly, though, we are very good at reading these signs in the faces of other people, even when they are trying to hide their true feelings. For example, we notice when a smile is not genuine, because the other person's eyes do not crinkle, or when a person who is pretending to be relaxed has a clenched jaw or a furrowed brow.

The Reward System

Although we have subtle ways of communicating through our body language, we are also capable of showing exactly how we feel very clearly! Think about some of your happiest memories. They probably include spending time with people you love, and showing them you love them, such as those warm cuddles from your mom or dad at bedtime, those close times with grandparents, and laughter with friends at school or on days off.

What is going on in our brain when we feel positive emotions such as love? It's all about rewards and pleasure. Deep in the brain is its reward system, a network of neurons that creates our sense of pleasure. Its purpose is to help us stay alive, by rewarding the behavior that is helpful for us with the experience of feeling great. So, for example, when we do something that is good for our survival, such as eating or drinking, it releases chemicals that flood across the neural network, creating a wave of pleasure. This motivates us to repeat the helpful behavior. One of the most common pleasure-giving chemicals is called dopamine. Its effect on us can be so powerful that people become addicted to it. They seek out situations that will stimulate their reward system to flood their brain with dopamine.

When we give someone a hug and tell them we love them, it releases dopamine in our brain, and also in theirs. So that warm, fuzzy feeling is not just imagined: It is actually a flood of pleasure-giving chemicals in the brain!

Thrill-Seekers

Scientists have studied how some people seem to be thrill-seekers. They love doing challenging and even dangerous things, such as parachuting or mountain climbing. Their reward system seems to have fewer brakes on it than most people's. It releases more dopamine than is usual, giving the person a greater sense of pleasure when they do something that gives them a feeling of achievement. This becomes addictive, so they look for more thrills.

SPEAK YOUR MIND

Can you think why it is good for our survival as a species to give and receive love? Back when we lived in small groups of hunter-gatherers, think about the benefits of creating social bonds between individuals and groups. How does giving and receiving love help us in the modern world? Give reasons for your answers.

Smiling and laughing with friends helps bond the group together—and makes us feel good!

Teenage Communication

Teenagers are not generally known for their ability to communicate. Sometimes, children who have been lively and always willing to talk to parents, teachers, or strangers may change around the age of 12 or 13. They may become much less communicative, change their body language, slouch, talk much less, and seem absorbed in a world inside their own head. What is going on in their brain?

As children grow into teenagers, their bodies begin to change in all kinds of ways. Some are easy to see, such as rapidly getting taller, but others are invisible. Inside their heads, their brains are beginning to change, too. These changes are preparing the young person for adult life, and while they are happening, things can get a little turbulent for a while. The brain has been developing an amazingly complex network of connections throughout childhood. Now, however, it begins to sort these out, to decide which ones are worth strengthening and which ones may not be needed in the future. A great "pruning" exercise begins. The result is a brain that is more efficient at doing the things that will be needed throughout adulthood.

Communication with parents can be tricky in your teenage years, as your brain goes through many changes.

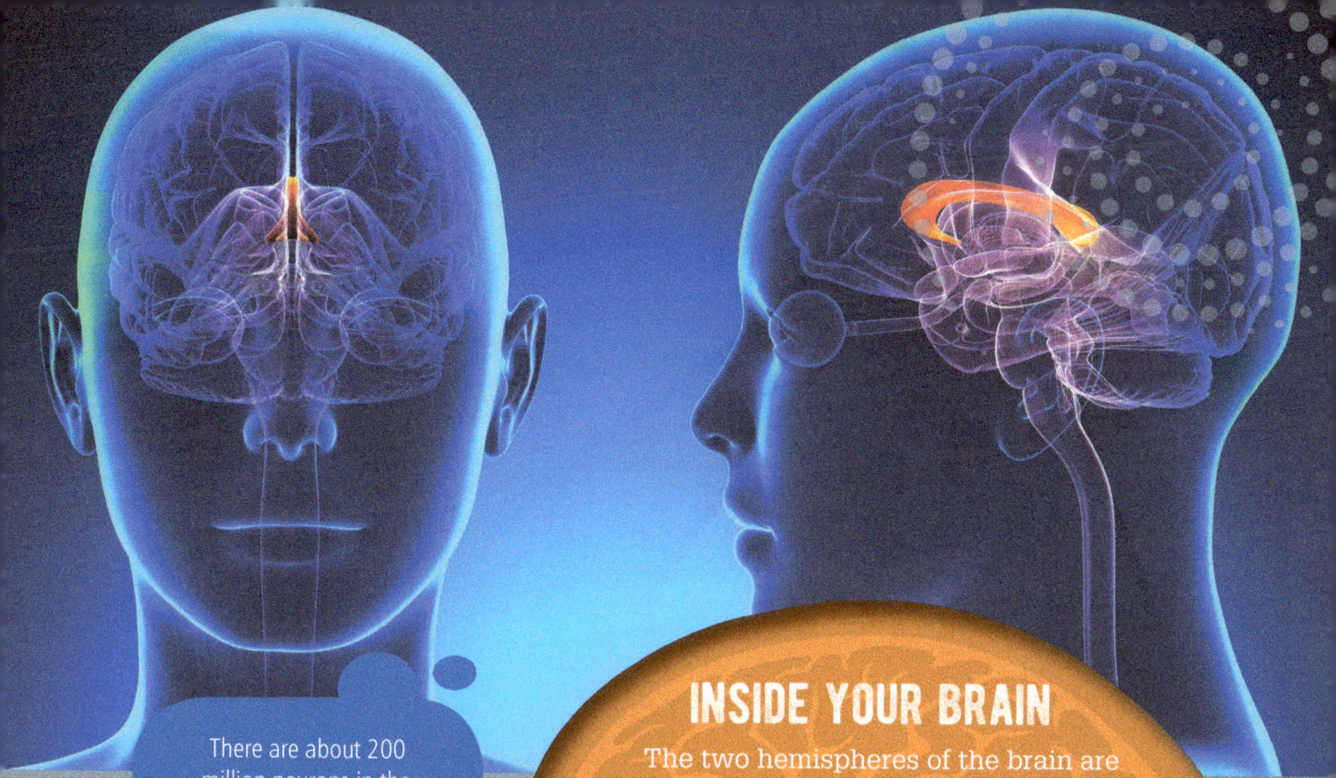

There are about 200 million neurons in the corpus callosum, connecting the two hemispheres of the brain.

INSIDE YOUR BRAIN

The two hemispheres of the brain are connected by a bundle of nerves called the corpus callosum. This becomes thicker during the teenage years, creating a stronger connection—and greater communication—between the right hemisphere, responsible for more creative thinking, and the left hemisphere, responsible for more of our language and number skills.

This process is exhausting! Teenagers need more sleep than adults, and find it difficult to get going in the morning. On the other hand, they may still be buzzing late into the night, when adults are wanting to sleep. As the areas of their brain develop and are pruned at different rates, their communication skills are affected. The areas of the brain responsible for emotion, in the limbic system, develop first, which can give teenagers some confusing feelings. Their mood may swing from high to low with little warning—and teenagers may feel unable not to express these emotions to the people around them quite vocally! The parts of the brain that deal with logical, careful thought, in the frontal lobe, develop later. This is why teenagers may seem unable to make rational decisions, to plan ahead, or to explain their behavior to others. Teens are also more likely to act and speak impulsively, and to take risks.

Laughing is actually good for you. It makes the brain release pleasure-giving chemicals that make you feel great!

Laughter

A joke is great at bringing people together, and it is amazing how similar people's senses of humor are around the world. It is a fantastic feeling to be in a movie theater laughing along with the rest of the audience at hilarious on-screen antics. When we hear a good joke, we naturally want to share it with our friends to make them laugh. But what exactly is this strange form of communication we call laughter?

Laughter is a basic instinct that all people share. We are born with the ability to laugh because it is in our genes. We do not consciously act out laughing—we just cannot help laughing! It turns out that laughter is a really useful form of communication. It creates bonds between people, and that makes life altogether safer and better. How often do you laugh at something funny when you are on your own? A good joke may make you smile to yourself, but actually we are much more likely to laugh out loud when we are with others than when we are alone.

Laughter is a powerfully positive means of communication. In an awkward social situation, laughter can help to ease the tension. The person making people laugh is playing a powerful role in bringing them together. Maybe that is why we value people who make us laugh so highly. Kids seem to know the power of laughter instinctively, too. When they are very young and are unsure about how to get along with other kids in preschool, for example, they often use laughing as a way of showing each other they want to make friends. The message is that they want to play together, not fight. The positive message laughter brings is understood by everyone.

What's So Funny?

What makes us laugh? Some comedy is physical: We find it funny when someone slips on a banana peel, or walks into a lamppost. In that situation we are really glad that it isn't us who is suffering. Sometimes jokes make us laugh because they have a big surprise at the end, in the punchline. Others are funny because they start by suggesting a dangerous situation, then bring relief when all turns out fine in the end. Relief often makes us laugh.

SPEAK YOUR MIND

Can you think of situations where we use the power of laughter in a negative way? Unfortunately, we have learned that this powerful tool can be used to hurt people as well as to bring them together. What does it feel like to be laughed at? Give reasons for your answers.

Long before their language skills are fully developed, young children use laughter to help make new friends.

Crying

We all have times when we feel sad, when we are hurt by something someone said or did, we are really worried about a situation, or we are in physical pain from an injury. Sadness, worry, and pain are really powerful emotions, and as humans we can communicate them in an equally powerful way: We burst into tears. What is crying, and where does it come from?

Humans seem to be the only species that cries tears as a form of communication. And what an effective communication tool it is! Just think of a newborn baby, unable to talk to explain their needs, but certainly able to cry. A baby uses crying to express many different feelings, from being hot or cold to being hungry, lonely, or uncomfortable. It is a challenge for any new parent to figure out what these cries mean, but it is almost impossible to ignore them altogether. We are "programmed" to respond to these powerful signals.

From birth to death, we cry to show sadness, and to ask for help. Crying is a reliable sign of our feelings, because it is very difficult to cry if you are not genuinely upset.

Crying in a joyful situation releases emotions and brings people closer together.

Asking for Help

Older children and adults also cry for a variety of reasons, from physical discomfort to the loss of a loved one or fear. How does crying help us? Although some people think crying is a sign of weakness, it is actually a sign of strength. We cry to tell others that we are having difficulty and we need help. Getting help when we need it makes us feel better, and strengthens the bonds between us and others. Even if you are alone, crying often makes you feel better. Sometimes, when harmful feelings build up, the brain tells us we need to cry to release them. We feel less stressed afterward, which is better for our health.

INSIDE YOUR BRAIN

Sometimes people cry not at sad or difficult things, but at happy ones! Your parents, for example, may cry when they see you on stage in the school play. What is going on there? This kind of crying is a release, too. The person crying is letting go of their defenses, revealing a deep emotion: their love for you. They probably cannot help it, however much you would like them not to embarrass you!

CHAPTER 6

SOCIAL COMMUNICATION

Music can be a powerful form of communication, helping people share and express their emotions.

Humans are naturally very social. We create social groups to live in to make our lives not only safer but enriched. These can be as small as a family of two or as large as a city—or the whole of the Internet! Even without understanding the languages of other countries, there are many other ways of communicating that are pretty much universal—they work just about anywhere.

Have you ever listened to a piece of music that made you feel like getting up and dancing? Or one that made you feel thoughtful, even sad? Music is just one of the results of our powerful human urge to be creative. Our creative brains produce an incredible range of wonderful things, from music, to dance, drama, and art. All of these things can communicate complex ideas and emotions to other people, sometimes without using language at all.

Relax for Inspiration

What is going on in the brain to produce all this creative output? You might think that our brains are working at their hardest when we are being most creative. Scientists measuring the electrical activity in the brain have found, surprisingly, that our brains seem to be most creative when they are relaxed and not hard at work. That fits with the experience many people have, of suddenly having a great idea when they thought they were just doing nothing, or were distracted by something else. Relaxing seems to give our brain the "space" it needs to think less logically and more instinctively or creatively. That is why it is really important to give yourself "down time" when you are not on your phone or working, but just letting your mind wander. That is when you are most likely to be inspired!

SPEAK YOUR MIND

The oldest cave paintings, probably made by Neanderthals, are believed to be more than 60,000 years old. The oldest known musical instruments, some bird bone and mammoth ivory flutes, are over 40,000 years old. What do you think early artists and musicians were trying to communicate to their tribes? Do you think their aims were similar to those of artists and musicians today? Why do you think humans are drawn to expressing themselves creatively? Give reasons for your answers.

These cave paintings in Argentina are about 9,000 years old. What message do you think the artists were trying to send?

There are few borders in the world of modern communications.

A World of Communications

We live in a highly connected world, a world where communication dominates our lives every day. This is mainly because of advances in technology over the past hundred years, such as radio, then television, then computers and the Internet. These things have made it possible for people around the world to communicate with one another in a split second. Sometimes it seems as if there are no remote corners of the world left. We have spread our communication network almost everywhere.

It is our brilliant brains that have allowed us to develop all this technology, and we use it to achieve some great things. People in poorer areas of the world, where the traditional communications network used to be very bad, can now be connected thanks to cell phone technology. They do not need an expensive infrastructure of cables and wires: They can use cheap, wireless cell phones to talk to friends and family, to contact the hospital, and to access news and information for learning and for work.

What Is the Impact?

Some people are worried, however, about the effect of all this communication technology on our brains. First, they wonder about the physical damage that holding a cell phone to your ear for long periods may do to your brain. Cell phones emit low doses of radio waves, and scientists are investigating carefully whether these may have a harmful effect on the brain. So far, the results of studies suggest that there may be a small risk, and that holding the phone away from your head, and not storing it in your pocket, is good practice.

The second impact of living in a world of constant communication is on our brain's health in a different way. Is it bad for us to be constantly bombarded with news and views—some of it frightening or abusive—on our phones, computers, and televisions, 24 hours a day? There is also plenty of evidence to suggest that social media creates huge pressure on people to be "perfect," to perform all the time, and that this can create enough stress to make people feel mentally unwell.

SPEAK YOUR MIND

Is it harmful for young people to be on social media all the time? It is great to be in touch with our friends, but do we also need time to be alone? Are there times when social media makes you feel lonelier rather than more connected? Give reasons for your answers.

Communication within a family can suffer when parents are always checking their emails and working during family time.

Computer Communication

We have used our brains to invent sophisticated and brilliant technology for communicating with one another. As a result we have "shrunk" the world, so that we can chat with someone thousands of miles away at the push of a button. We have created computers that can perform some tasks much, much better than we can. They can process huge amounts of data in a split second, far more efficiently than our brains could ever manage, then send the information down wires to another computer on the other side of the Atlantic Ocean. However, could a computer ever become as good a communicator as the human brain?

Artificial Intelligence

The area of artificial intelligence (AI) is one of the most exciting and controversial areas of science and technology today. Artificial intelligence is where a computer seems to "think for itself," without being told to perform every task by a human operator. However, artificial intelligence is, in fact, created by the very complex programming of very powerful computers. Computer scientists have been trying for decades to create computers that have AI by programming them with sets of rules called "algorithms," which allow computers to carry out logical reasoning.

Scientists are also building computers that are structured like brains, with "neural" networks of artificial brain cells, just like the neural networks

Could AI develop an artificial brain that works like a human one, with all its awesome complexity?

Headsets that scan the brain's electrical activity have the potential to tell scientists so much more about this most extraordinary organ.

in real brains. When you feed information into these networks, over and over, the computers gradually learn to recognize patterns and make connections. Having learned this information and stored it in a memory, the computer can use what it has learned to make decisions in new situations. It has learned to "think for itself" and then can communicate the results of its reasoning to other computers or its human user. However, since much of human communication is not logical but instinctive, could a computer ever truly be as good a communicator as a human?

INSIDE YOUR BRAIN

There are now toys and gadgets that we can control using the communication power of our brains. The user wears a headset that detects the electrical activity of neurons in several areas of their brain, and translates those signals into commands, which it sends to the device. Maybe one day soon we will be able to type on our computers just by thinking the words we want to say! At the moment, these mind-controlled toys are just fun, but one day soon they could have the power to really help people, such as those with disabilities.

AMAZING COMMUNICATION

We live in a world where communication is key. As the most intelligent species on our planet, we have developed the most amazing ways to communicate with one another. We have the gift of language, a complex system of sounds that we use to create a code of words with meaning. This has allowed us to pass on to one another the things we have learned over hundreds of thousands of years, so that we have built a highly developed civilization.

We are born with the capacity to learn the skills of language, to speak our native language and others, to read, and to write.

Powerful communicators, such as Martin Luther King Jr., can use words even to bring about changes in society. His moving "I Have a Dream" speech could not have been written by a computer.

Our brains are also hardwired to communicate with people in nonverbal ways, through the universally understood signals of body language and facial expression. We can also use our creativity to communicate with each other through music, and through the visual arts of painting, drawing, and sculpture. The popularity of the arts around the world shows how very highly we value these methods of communication.

So Much to Learn

Over the past century, scientists have learned an immense amount about how the brain works, but there is still much we do not understand. We cannot cut open a living brain to see what it is doing. We rely on scans to show us the brain areas that are active during different activities. This makes it very difficult to understand the complexities of diseases of the brain, or why some humans struggle with communication. We do not yet know how much of what happens in our brains is inherited, determined by our genes, and how much is the result of things that happen to us in life. One thing is certain: that scientists will continue to use their brainpower to advance their knowledge, and to communicate what they know to the rest of us, so that we can all grow in understanding.

INSIDE YOUR BRAIN

At the moment, no scientist has created an artificial brain or computer that has the complexity and variety of powers of the human brain. The communication pathways inside our brains are incredibly sophisticated, because we use so many different kinds of signals in our interactions with others to inform our behavior. We look at others' body language, we speak and listen to them, and we relate what we see and hear to our past experiences with other people. It will take one awesome robot to be able to do all that!

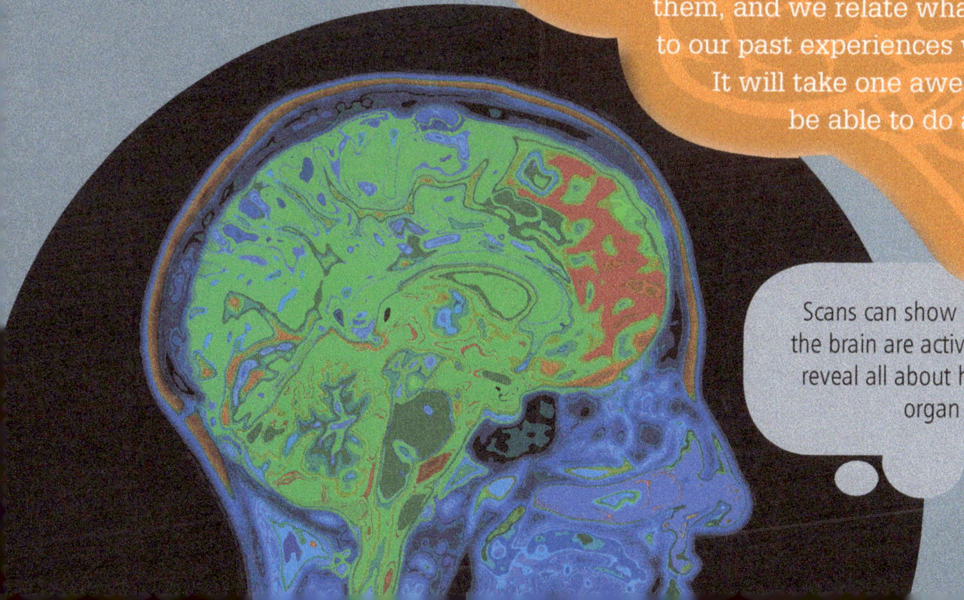

Scans can show us which areas of the brain are active, but they cannot reveal all about how this powerful organ works.

GLOSSARY

amygdala The area of the brain that deals with emotions.

artificial intelligence (AI) Computer programs that are able to learn from experience.

bilingual Able to speak two languages equally fluently.

Braille A system of raised dots representing letters and words, which people who are blind read with their fingers.

brain stem The part of the base of the brain that controls our heartbeat and breathing.

cells The building blocks of life; different types of cells are specialized to carry out different tasks in the body.

cerebellum The area at the back of the brain that controls the working of our muscles and the heart.

cerebral cortex The outside layer of the brain that is used for many key functions.

corpus callosum A bundle of nerve fibers that connects the two hemispheres of the brain.

developmental language disorder (DLD) A disorder that affects children's ability to understand and use spoken language.

dopamine A chemical released in the brain that makes us feel pleasure.

dyslexia A learning disorder that affects the ability to connect letters with sounds.

genes The parts of every cell that determine some of our characteristics.

hemispheres Halves of a sphere; the two halves of the brain.

intuition The feeling of knowing or understanding something without having been told it.

limbic system A group of parts of the brain that deals with our sense of smell, memory, and emotions.

lobes Each hemisphere of the brain is divided into four lobes: the frontal, parietal, occipital, and temporal.

nervous system The body's network of neurons in nerves and the brain.

neurons Nerve cells.

neuroscientists Scientists who study the brain and the nervous system.

phonemes The smallest units of sound in reading.

stroke When the blood supply to the brain is temporarily cut off.

FOR MORE INFORMATION

Books

Abramovitz, Melissa. *Brain Science*. Minneapolis, MN: Essential Library, 2016.

Drimmer, Stephanie Warren. *Brain Bogglers*. Washington, DC: National Geographic, 2017.

Smibert, Angie. *Artificial Intelligence: Thinking Machines and Smart Robots with Science Activities for Kids*. White River Junction, VT: Nomad Press, 2018.

Winterberg, Jena. *Sound Waves and Communication*. Huntington Beach, CA: Teacher Created Materials, 2015.

Websites

Find out more about the brain at:
brainmadesimple.com

Read entertaining facts about the brain at:
www.coolkidfacts.com/facts-about-the-brain-for-kids

View a helpful diagram and read about what happens inside the brain at:
www.dkfindout.com/us/human-body/brain-and-nerves/inside-brain

Learn more about the brain and its parts at:
www.ducksters.com/science/brain.php

INDEX